MICHAEL DONA

wallflowers

a lecture on poetry with misplaced
notes and additional heckling

THE POETRY SOCIETY

First published in 1999
by The Poetry Society

Design/layout by Stephen Troussé at The Poetry Society
Printed by Grillford Ltd, Milton Keynes

ISBN 1 900771 14 4

Poetry Places

IN 1997 THE Poetry Society received a grant from the 'Arts for Everyone' budget of the Arts Council of England Lottery Department for an innovative scheme to bring poetry to new audiences. This two-year programme of residencies, placements and projects explores the unique role that poetry can play in different settings. So far, more than eighty poets have been involved in projects ranging from forests, fish and chip shops and festivals to museums, parks and even an off-shore gas platform.

At Marks and Spencer, Peter Sansom visited stores around the country and ran workshops for staff from directors to sales assistants. At law firm Mischon de Reya, Lavinia Greenlaw stimulated an e-mail correspondence about poetry with people who hadn't read a poem since they left school. At London Zoo, Tobias Hill created a poetry trail and read poems in the Aquarium. Sarah Maguire planted a poetry garden at Chelsea Physic Garden; Gary Boswell put poems on bin bags in North Norfolk; David Hart responded to the life and history of Worcester Cathedral and Jackie Wills explored poetry as a land-use planning tool in the Surrey Hills.

Poets have worked with drug users, sex offenders, lawyers, executives, teachers, children and workers of all kinds as well as with poetry enthusiasts around the country. As Creative Reader in Residence for Poetry Places, Michael Donaghy has brought wit and intelligence to a scheme remarkable for its breadth and diversity.

CHRISTINA PATTERSON
POETRY PLACES CO-ORDINATOR, MAY 1999

Cuis rei demonstrationem mirabilem sane dextei hanc marginis exiguitas non caparet.*

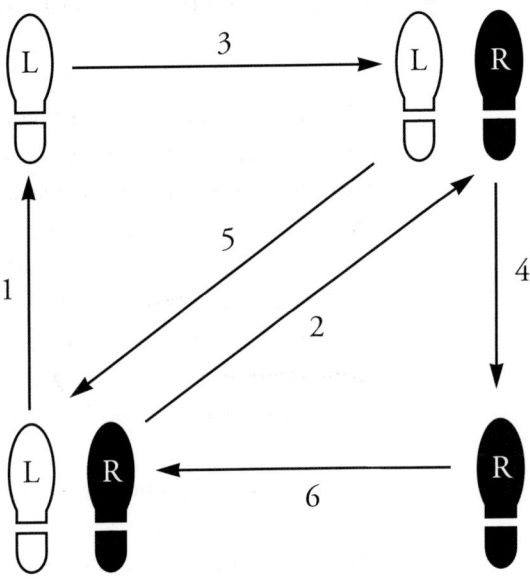

* I have a truly marvellous demonstration of this proposition which this margin is too narrow to contain.
                         – Fermat

1 Telling the Dancer from the Dance

ALL MY LIFE I have harboured a weakness for those wilfully eccentric philosophical and theological precepts valuable for their beauty alone, like Swedenborg's fancy that, in their purity and self-lessness, angels create space instead of taking it up, thereby dilating the pin upon which they dance, or the North African Gnostic idea that all material beings are 3D letters in the penmanship of God, or the Cabalistic fear that when, in the next great age, the Hebrew letter *shin* grows a fourth vertical stroke, a new sound will utter from men's mouths, making pronounceable the hitherto unpronounceable name of God – at which precise moment the world will end.

    Having thus disqualified myself from from the role of earnest philosopher, I'd like to share with you my own homely addition to this aviary of ideas, a minor epiphany concerning the relationship of the poet and the reader... This idea occurred to me one rainy night about twenty years ago in a church hall on the south side of Chicago.

    ...I'd been playing jigs and reels for a *ceilidh*, watching the set dancers spinning and stamping out with wild precision the rhythms of a dance which can be described (accurately) as a feral minuet. Sometime during the course of the evening the music I had for years only heard and played became visible, filled with spinning sweaty couples, as the abstract shape of a whirlpool fills with water, or an equation takes shape as a tetrahedron. Only after

---

Reader in Residence:
Your attention, please. This is not a digression. This is your representative jotting a note in the margin on your behalf. Imagine for a moment that you are not merely reading this note, but thinking in these very words as you read them and our task will be much easier. We think Mr Donaghy is about to be extravagant, anecdotal, and self-dramatising.

My uncle Jack Sheehy, traditional musician, the Bronx, 1955.

the dancers had left the floor did I notice the circular patterns of black scuffs and streaks their heels had made on the polished wood.

This pattern, I recognised, was an enormous encoded page of poetry, a kind of manuscript, or, more properly, a *pediscript*.

If I were standing before you saying this, you wouldn't have to read it. These lines are instructions for your voice to mimic mine (you may not be moving your lips as you read, but your breath and throat muscles are changing subtly in response). Just as a manuscript is a set of rules for summoning the speaker (from beyond the grave, if necessary), the pediscript is a set of rules for executing the dance.

In order to interpret that dance chart you've got to get up and move (imagine describing a spiral staircase with your hands behind your back, or a chess game without a board and pieces). But your dance partner is long gone. All that remains is a diagram, or the black streaks on the floorboards.

Like all literary poetry in our culture, the pediscript is the record of – or formula for – a social transaction, all that remains of that give and take between artist and participating audience in an oral tradition. It's not my intention here to underrate or dismiss the enormous intellectual advantage in being a wallflower at that dance. But the wordless dialogue of dancers and musicians in the dance hall, the dancer's relationships with one another... Over that next year or so, I began to compare that order of experience, *bodily* experience, with my academic experience of poetry.

This was 1977. Then as now, the term 'tradition' was politically charged for academics and intellectuals. For them it suggested orthodoxy, exclusivity, and their own disputed canon of prescribed

masterpieces of European culture. But I grew up among several communities of immigrants in New York City – Italian, Irish, Puerto Rican – who regarded their oral traditions as a covenant with their respective cultures. A player in such a tradition is expected to improvise, to 'make it new', and the possibilities for expression within the prescribed forms are infinite. But it's considered absurd to violate the conventions of the form, the 'shape' of the dance tune or story, because you leave the community of your audience behind, and you bring the dancers to a standstill. By 'traditional form' I mean the shape of the dance, those verbal and rhythmical schemes shared by the living community which link it to the dead and to generations to come.[1] I'm not making a distinction between 'form' as that word applies to, say, iambic pen-

---

[1] Before writing existed, the only way to transmit important information from one generation to the next was to cast it in a memorisable form, to make it a song, for example, or a ritual dance, and this is still the case in cultures that have no written language. Systems for memorising data are called mnemonics after Mnemosyne, the muse of memory, and these systems provide a clue to the origins of poetry. Rhyme, for example, is one such technique. How many days are in April? Before answering, most people instinctively run through the rhyme 'Thirty days have September, April, June and November...'. Spell 'receive': '"i" before "e" except after "c"'. Another common technique is to associate units of information with words in a sentence. What are the notes on the musical scale? Most novice musicians remember that 'Every Good Boy Deserves Favour'. Yet another way involves the use of imagery; paired items, an angel and a crown, say, can be learned more rapidly if they're associated in a simple sentence – the angel is given the crown. The best way is to make pairs of items interact in some way – the angel dons the crown – and then link those items with a third, the crowned angel unfurls a scroll, and keep the chain going. In mnemonics, stories are often spun out of the need to remember the images they contain – in literature it's often the other way round.

The 'forms' to which I refer here are shapes, like the 'schemes' of classical rhetoric – *parachesis*, *hypophora*, etc – the artificial patterning of words, as opposed to 'tropes' like imagery. We must distinguish between memorability and memorisability. A rhyme or rhythm makes a point memorisable; a slap across the face (like a 'striking' image) makes anything memorable. In the absence of working schemes, artists have to slap a lot of face to have any noticeable effect.[1a]

[1a] The footnote is my voice, of course, but in a slightly hushed tone, to distinguish it from the body of my argument.

tameter and the form of a twelve bar Blues, or a Petrarchan sonnet and a playground skipping rhyme.

If we were discussing this in person, I'd roll up the carpet and illustrate my point by marking out a diagram on the floor. But first let's consider just what a diagram is. It's a schematic picture, certainly, like a graph, a map, or a geometric proof, and we all accept nowadays that pictures are highly conventional, no matter how naturalistic they may appear at first glance. It's said that Picasso was once challenged by a model's husband who complained that the picture he'd painted bore little resemblance to his wife. 'What does she look like?' asked Picasso. The man took a snapshot from his wallet. Picasso squinted and said 'She's very small isn't she?' And, of course, he might have added that she was two-dimensional, monochrome, motionless, cut off at the waist, and that only the tip of her nose was truly in focus. Like the model's husband, we're tempted to accept pictorial conventions as natural, and our senses of scale and perspective, even our sense of beauty, are often modified by the conventions of image-making.

Maps and blueprints are pictures too. They function as instruments to help us to construct buildings or find our way through a city or forest by omitting most of the detail in order to emphasise the relation of a few relevant parts. And sometimes the conventions are relatively easy to spot. We know, for example, that a map is usually an aerial view with north at the top of the map and west to the left. We all know that when we look at a map on a wall we don't go north by flying straight up to the ceiling. The map of the London Underground is very useful in getting from A to B, but Londoners know it's worse than useless for getting about on the surface. And certainly no one expects a house to resemble a blueprint. Geometrical proofs are a special case. These are the only diagrams that don't distort because they operate on the level of the ideal, purged of the noise of the real world. So geometry is pure diagram: the scheme or shape of a triangle or square or circle defined by a 'key' or 'legend' of equations using arbitrary markers – what mathematicians call 'variables'.[2]

But when the diagram represents a process unfolding in *time* the hazards of oversimplification in any picture are even more insidious because the conventions of the picture can't be checked against the visible, tangible, apparently stable world. When, for example, we see a diagram depicting species 'developing' in branches from the root of a schematic tree, we're slipped a specious subliminal message beneath this visual metaphor, that living species are 'higher' than extinct species and somehow superior to them when in fact evolution is a response to arbitrary environmental changes ('the survival of the fittest' may be better expressed as 'the survival of the survivors'). This dubious message, that the rudimentary past is somehow perfected into the present, underpinned the Victorian notion of 'progress' and figures in a lot of 20th century ideas about art and literature.

Or consider the illusions built into that animated diagram of time itself, the clock face. Every day we experience both the use-

---

[2] Michael Serres has a beautiful and fantastic hypothesis about the origin of geometry: Democritus and Plato both say the Greeks crossed the sea to educate themselves in Egypt. The problem, of course, is that the Egyptians wrote in the ideograms of hieroglyphics and the Greeks used an alphabet, a system of arbitrary signs to represent sounds. Geometry, he says, originated in the blending of these two systems of writing into a game in which they are utterly interdependent and describe nothing but each other. The square, triangle and circle, he says, are all that remains in Greece of hieroglyphics.

fulness of clocks and watches and their utter inadequacy in representing our real experience of duration. That last hour in bed with your lover and the next hour waiting for the night bus in the rain are only the same to your watch. Whenever we speak of 'Time', that abstract generalisation covering the infinite variety of change taking place all around us, we speak in simple spatial metaphors; we say, for example, that it 'moves forward' and it was until recently commonly expressed that some cultures were 'backward'. Even our self-perception is informed by the diagram; models of the mind from Associationism to Freud and Jung depend on visualisable diagrams of mental processes. Even in our ordinary use of words like introspection we locate consciousness inside our heads. We imagine a roomy mental arena, which we usually locate inside our brains, though other cultures have placed it in the heart or the guts. But a close look at our terms reveals this as just another spatial illusion. You can 'see where this is leading'. I'm 'approaching' a 'deep' problem, one I've kept at 'the back of my mind'.

In non-literate cultures, of course, the only way to preserve knowledge is to make it memorisable,[3] and the most efficient way to do this is to render that knowledge into a mental pattern – an invisible dance which only comes alive with the participation of an

---

[3] Aboriginal Australians believe that their ancestors sung the world into existence during their walkabout in the Dream Time and that the world's existence can only be maintained by keeping faith with tradition – going walkabout and navigating by singing the 'songlines' (footnotes like this are a matter of creative juxtaposition. Gilbert Watts, in his English version of *De Augmentis Scientarum* (1640) inveighed against the other sort of footnote or marginal note, the citation of authorities:

...as if the Truth they deliver were to be tried by voices; or having lost its primitive innocence, must be covertd with these fig leaves; or as if the Authors themselves were afraid that it should make an escape out of the text, were it not beset in the Margin with Authorities as with a watch.

Wallflowers again).

audience. This even holds true for classical oratory. From antiquity to the Renaissance, the rhetorical art of memory entailed the committing to memory of real or imaginary buildings such as temples, law courts, or cathedrals. A speaker could commit to memory, for example, the four virtues, the seven deadly sins, or a list of Roman emperors, by associating each in succession with the fixed parts of the building. To facilitate this feat of memorisation, each part of the building would be equipped with a highly symbolic figure or striking image, to help fix the point for both the speaker and the audience. The individual alcoves or columns were known as the rooms or places, and this comes down to us today in expressions like 'topics' of conversation (from *topoi*, place); a 'commonplace' meaning a cliché; or in the *stanza* – Italian, room – of a poem.[4] *Strophe*, another kind of stanza, described a dance in the Greek choral ode, the chorus pacing in one direction chanting the strophe and back again chanting the antistrophe, arranging the parts of the song in theatrical space.

With this in mind – and the front of your mind will serve as well as the back – consider how any printed page of verse or prose, with all its paraphernalia of paragraphs, running heads, marginalia, pagination, footnotes, titles, line breaks and stanzas, can be understood as a diagram of a mental process.[5] And consider how much more insidious or convincing those conventions are when the dia-

---

[4] Donne alludes to this kind of poetic space in 'The Canonisation':

> We can die by it, if not live by love,
> And if unfit for tombs and hearse
> Our legend be, it will be fit for verse;
> And if no piece of Chronicle we prove,
> We'll build in sonnets pretty rooms;
> As well a well wrought urn becomes
> The greatest ashes, as half-acre tombs,
> And by these hymns, all shall approve
> Us Canonised for Love.

gram itself is invisible – I mean this as no airy metaphor: the words in the centre of the page surrounded by their somewhat reserved audience of footnotes and marginalia are a diagram of self consciousness, a commentary frozen out of the flow of the story, song, or poem, out of the voice we've entered as we participate. In the extremest sense, the sense of the oral tradition, of the centre of gravity of all poetry, the sense of children's bedtime stories and ritual dramas like *Oedipus Rex* or the Mass, the audience are participants in total immersion, surrendering consciousness and voice to the story. But to read critically, as poetry readers do, alone in bed, or at their desks, or huddled together around the workshop table – wallflowers – is to scribble in the margin. The page encourages an illusion and seduces us with its model of the mind.

First digression

In 1798 Wordsworth and Coleridge, weary of some of the literary conventions of their day, invoked a different, perhaps more mannered set of oral conventions in their *Lyrical Ballads*. Coleridge's opening contribution to the volume was 'The Rime of the Ancyent Marinere' – to all appearances an hallucinatory, ergot-fuelled 16th century ballad drawn from Gothic Romance, *The Arabian Nights*, and Renaissance travel books. There's a Latin epigraph from Burnet, an 'Argument', and then we're right into the thick of the tale.

---

[5] And sure enough, our word diagram derives from διαγραμμα, which doesn't distinguish between a geometrical figure fixing the relation of parts from a written list.

> It is an ancyent Marinere,
> And he stoppeth one of three:
> 'By thy long grey beard and thy glittering eye
> 'Now wherefore stoppest me?
> 'The Bridegroom's doors are open'd wide
> 'And I am next of kin;
> 'The Guests are met, the Feast is set, –
> 'May'st hear the merry din.

This is, in other words, the story of the story. The wedding guest could well be the reader's representative or listener in residence.

> But still he holds the wedding-guest –
> There was a Ship, quoth he –
> 'Nay, if thou'st got a laughsome tale,
> 'Marinere! come with me'.
> He holds him with his skinny hand,
> Quoth he, there was a Ship –
> 'Now get thee hence, thou grey-beard Loon!
> 'Or my Staff shall make thee skip.
> He holds him with his glittering eye –
> The wedding guest stood still
> And listens like a three year's child;
> The Marinere hath his will.
> The wedding-guest sate on a stone,
> He cannot chuse but hear:
> And thus spake on that ancyent man,
> The bright-eyed Marinere.

Seventeen years later Coleridge presented a new version in Sybylline Leaves. Alongside the outermost margins of the open book there now appeared a marginal commentary, a pastiche of a 17th century gloss, like evidence from which the reader deduces the presence of an imaginary scholar explicating the imaginary poet of a story of a story being told.

An Ancient	It is an ancyent Marinere,
Mariner meeteth	And he stoppeth one of three:
three Gallants	'By thy long grey beard and thy glittering eye
bidden to a	'Now wherefore stoppest me?
wedding feast,	'The Bridegroom's doors are open'd wide
and detaineth	'And I am next of kin;
one.	'The Guests are met, the Feast is set, –
	'May'st hear the merry din.

A brilliant stroke! Coleridge has interposed another reader between us and the text, and found a use for all that blank space in the left hand margin.

It was Coleridge who introduced the term *marginalia* to English from Latin. Some Coleridge scholar ought to consider the way Coleridge used peripheries – introductions, margins and footnotes. From the introductory anecdote to 'Kubla Khan' to the grand hypertext of his *Biographia Literaria*, Coleridge exploited the physical space of the printed book to point up its illusions and suggest the living presence behind the words.

End of digression

Mr Donaghy is gently moving us into position. Is this where we're supposed to stand?

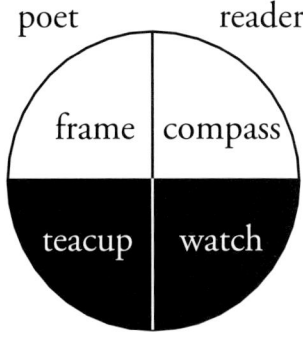

Are we being insulted?

Duly cautioned as to the treachery of diagrams, let's move on to my own. Let this blackboard represent the dance floor. Just as musicians play for dancers, poets write for readers (or listeners) so let these two be our leading couple.

For the poet (upper left) form functions as a kind of 'frame' or 'scaffold' from which the poem can be constructed. Stravinsky maintained that only in art could one be freed by the imposition of more rules, perhaps because these rules limit the field of possibilities and escort us beyond the selection of tools and media to laying the first stone of the work itself (of course, once the basic structure is built, rooms, *stanzas*, can be altered from the inside).

For the reader (upper right), the shared language of the poem functions as a compass or map to assist us through the terrain of a new idea. Traditionally, narratives or arguments are parsed into, for example, episodes in which three wishes are granted, or rhetorical points explored. Physical expressions like 'On the one hand...' warn the listener to bracket the ensuing information and prepare for its antithesis '...and on the other...'. These phrases exploit the reader's or audience's expectations, which, on a larger scale, is the aspect of tradition routinely targeted by the avant garde in this passing century as vulgar, bourgeois and tranquillising.[6]

So much for the conscious operation of these schemes. Now

---

[6] Another aspect of audience expectation is the display of *conspicuous, publicly perceptible effort* and mastery of form – tacit agreements in the freat unwritten contract between artist and audience. In Renaissance Italy the master painter, sculptor, dancer, musician or poet was an *Amatore delle defficulta* – lover of difficulties. Lorenzo de Medici, for example praised the form of the sonnet 'arguing from its difficulty – since noble accomplishment (*virtù*), according to the philosophers, consists in the difficult'. Nor is the familiar popular reaction to modern painting and poetry – 'my five year old can draw better' and 'it doesn't rhyme' – the exclusive reserve of philistines who value over Picasso, say, scale models of cathedrals made from matchsticks. Modernist critics and literary historians also regard laborious and time-consuming composition as evidence of artistic integrity.

Attention. We are considering the effect of this image: Mr Donaghy is holding up a watch. It resembles the hypnotist's dangling fob watch familiar from end-of-the-pier shows and B movies ("Your eyes are getting heavy").

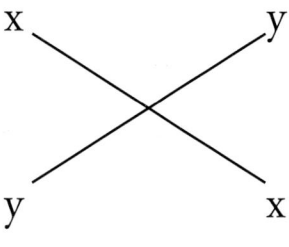

let's look below the surface, to something I find far more mysterious, the unconscious or subliminal effects of reading and writing in traditional form. The unconscious effect of form on the reader I identify by the icon of the watch.[7]

We are hypnotised or spellbound by form because the traditional aural techniques of verse, the mnemonics of rhyme, metre, and rhetorical schemes, are designed to fix the poem in the memory, to burn it in deeper than prose. And because it stays in the memory a split second longer, because it '*sounds* right', it seems to *be* right. Advertising copywriters and political speech writers know this, and take advantage of those venerable schemes of classical rhetoric to convince us below the level of reason, to sell us fags or governments.

Take *chiasmus*, for example: At John F. Kennedy's inauguration Robert Frost was scheduled to read his poem 'The Gift Outright' which began with the lines 'The land was ours before we were the land's....Possessing what we still were unpossessed by, / Possessed by what we now no more possessed'. Shortly afterwards, Kennedy's own speech contained the calculatedly memorable line 'Ask not what your country can do for you. Ask what you can do for your country'. The content of Kennedy's sentence is political propaganda, Frost's 'a momentary stay against confusion', but both share the familiar shape of 'Beauty is truth, truth beauty' like a dance step in which two couples change partners – never mind that beauty and

---

[7]   Beyond the name there lies what has no name;
Today I have felt its shadow stir the aim
Of this blue needle, light and keen, whose sweep

Homes to the utmost of the sea its love,
Suggestive of a watch in dreams, or of
Some bird, perhaps, who shifts a bit in sleep.
From 'The Compass', Borges, trans Wilbur.

truth can only be identical from a viewpoint shared by God, Grecian urns and mathematicians. Or consider the appealing symmetry of 'An eye for an eye and a tooth for a tooth' – hardly a useful sentiment in the late 20th century, but the rhetorical shape seems to validate and mask as an allegorical figure of *Justitia* our base instinct for revenge.

These formulae are the verbal equivalent of the pictorial space of the diagram and, as such, they are equally insidious. Les Murray has said that rhyme functions with the symmetry of logic. The terrifying truth is that form *substitutes* for logic. This is the poet's unique power, to address the passions in their own language, the very power that got us barred from the *Republic*.

Finally, let's consider the unconscious effect of form on the poet. This is the most interesting aspect of traditional technique, and it represents the intervention of that presence poets used to call 'The Muse'. Any degree of difficulty in a form requires of the poet that he or she negotiate with the medium, and compromise what he or she originally 'spontaneously' intended to say (so far so good, since one's instantaneous reaction is always more likely to be full of self-deception, prejudice and cliché).[8] Perhaps many of us here have experienced the peculiar sensation that the best image or line simply 'came to us' as if delivered by an unseen presence as a

---

[8] Leonardo criticised the painters, who, as he put it, 'want even the slightest trace of charcoal to remain valid', and asked them: 'Have you never thought about how poets compose their verse? They never trouble to trace beautiful letters nor do they mind crossing out several lines to improve them'. He wanted to warn artists to keep their compositions 'provisional' until they hit upon a radiant form, and warns against a method which would tie their creative process down to the original commitment. He advises the painters that they should 'be ready to change course at any moment, like the poet'. I for one have never ascertained how long I have to think of something before it stops being spontaneous. Perhaps it's not a matter of duration. Perhaps true spontaneity takes its own time.

17

reward for taking the time to work hard on a poem. It comes from our own unconscious, of course. The feeling of 'otherness' is explained by the fact that our self-perception is firmly rooted in our waking consciousness.[9]

I represent this aspect of form with, of all things, a teacup. I'm alluding here to the late American poet James Merrill who, like Yeats, claimed to have contacted and drawn on the assistance of 'the other side'. In the opening scene of his supernatural epic *The Changing Light At Sandover*, Merrill and his partner are playing about with a Ouija board. Suddenly, the upturned teacup they've been using for a pointer is commandeered by the soul of one of Caligula's murdered slaves. The spirit, Ephraim, answers their questions instantly, and largely in rhyme and metre. Later, Merrill refers to the attraction of the 'bedevilling couplet' and it's clear to this reader, at least, that Merrill's supernatural familiars are in part metaphors for the shaping forces of verse technique. John Ashbery has used a more mechanical metaphor to describe this effect 'The really bizarre requirements of a sestina', he told *New York Quarterly*, 'I use as a probing tool rather than as a form in the traditional sense... rather like riding downhill on a bicycle and having the pedals push your feet. I wanted my feet pushed into places they wouldn't

---

[9] See 'The Feeling of a Presence and Verbal Meaningfulness in Context of Temporal Lobe Function: Factor Analytic Verification of the Muses?' Persinger, Michael, A; Marakerec, Katherine, *Brain and Cognition*, 1992, November, Vol 20 (2): 217-226. Persinger and Makrakerec hypothesize that the profound sensation of a presence, particularly during periods of profound verbal creativity in reading or writing prose or poetry is an endemic cognitive phenomenon. Factor analyses of 12 clusters of phenomenological experiences from 348 men and 520 women (aged 18-65 years), who enrolled in undergraduate psychology courses over a ten year period, supported the hypothesis. The authors conclude that periods of intense meaningfulness (a likely correlate of enhanced burst-firing in the left hippoclampal-amygdaloid complex and temporal lobe) allow access to nonverbal representations that are the right hemispheric equivalents of the sense of self: they are perceived as a presence [from the Abstract].

I really must object on the reader's behalf. We've spent valuable time and energy visualising Mr Donaghy's diagram and now he sees fit to erase it.

normally have taken'. But surely this is *precisely* the function of 'form in the traditional sense' that serendipity provided by negotiation with a resistant medium.

I began by warning against the dangers of simplification inherent in all diagrams, so I ought to dismantle my own. Any act of communication begins with imagining oneself in the place of potential readers or listeners in order to anticipate one's effect. Agreed? It could be said, then, that the poet *equals* the reader, because poets are themselves readers in the tradition of poetry, because poetry is in itself a way of reading in that tradition, and because poets are the first (and sometimes, sadly, the only) readers and critics of what they've written. Conversely, reading is a form of ventriloquism: sensitive readers give themselves up to the poet for the duration of the poem. (The night I watched those dancers in Chicago I realised the same relationship obtained in other traditional arts. When a *shannachie*, or traditional storyteller, spins his long tales, the reaction of the listening audience is part of the event, just as the reaction of the dancers complements and completes the music. As Borges says in his essay on Shaw, the poem is properly a dialogue with the reader and the peculiar accent he gives to its voice, the changing and durable images it leaves in his memory. That dialogue, he says, is infinite.)

So my diagram is really a kind of equation, and the condition of all equations is the resolution to equality of terms on either side of the equal sign.[10] It follows then that the frame or scaffolding of form is really no different from the compass and map of our own

---

[10] 'Pronouns in poetry are like the "x" in algebra. Much of the enjoyment of reading certain poems involves the "solving" of the poem/equation's values for "I" and "U"' – Thom Disch.

expectations as readers. And the spell induced by the hypnotist's fob watch, that power of subliminal persuasion, is the same spell the Muse exerts over our own imaginations.

Certainly poetry can address our rational side, but just as it gets its power from a place beyond reason, it affords us the power to address, represent, or exploit that same dangerous territory. Surely, one of our duties as twenty-first century readers and poets will be to explore the political, however personal or oblique our approach, and that exploration will require questioning, dubiety, speculation, analysis. But as poets we have that unique power to address the passions in their own language. Perhaps our challenge , as we gradually leave the age of print, will be to discharge our writerly, civic duties from this platform without bringing to a standstill those rapt, whirling dancers just visible beyond the glare of the stagelights – amongst whom we might just glimpse ourselves.

2 Reading in rhythm

NOT LONG AGO I found myself engaged in a curious and ambitious translation project with a number of deaf poets who composed in sign language. By way of introduction to their craft they showed me a photocopy of a poem by the American deaf poet Clayton Valli. I was acutely embarrassed by the apparent mediocrity of the work and I when I asked my signing interpreter to rescue me from this diplomatic disaster, she suggested we watch a video of Valli performing the poem in American Sign Language (ASL). It was extraordinarily beautiful and a clear example of Frost's dictum 'poetry is what's lost in translation' for this performance was the poem. The photocopied sheet on my lap was no more a work of literary art than a choreographer's stage directions can be said to constitute a ballet, or a pediscript a pavane.

'How can we tell the dancer from the dance?' Yeats asks in 'Among School Children', to which the uncowed reader may respond 'why try?'. And here it seemed equally pointless to separate the poem from the bodily presence of the poet. The signed poem rides on the carrier wave of the signing poet's bodily rhythm and uses regular repetition of glance, nod, handshape, headshake, and innumerable other subtle physical signals the way audible verse uses rhymes or refrains. 'Silence' is a slight pause, or a long freeze at the conclusion of a context. Signed poetry establishes its artificiality, its departure from conversational signing, by conscious grace; often the poet breaks eye contact, slows down, and divides

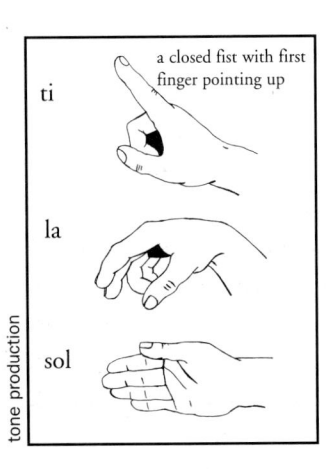

Zoltan Kodaly's Sol-Fa system of gestures for tone production

ti — a closed fist with first finger pointing up

la

sol

Neumes?

Pardon?

signing between both hands for visual balance – broadly speaking, by returning language to dance.

The historian R.G. Collingwood, who called dance 'the mother of language', recognised that all language is rooted in the fact of bodily presence.

> We get still farther away from the fundamental facts about speech when we think of it as something that can be written and read, forgetting that writing, in our clumsy notations, can represent only a small part of the spoken sound, where pitch and stress, where tempo and rhythm, are almost entirely ignored... The written or printed book is only a series of hints, as elliptical as the neumes of Byzantine music.

Why, 'neumes' are those little strokes indicating pitch and vocal ornament accompanying the chants in ancient missals. Neumes were the predecessors of modern musical notes, originally Greek textual accents that were gradually modified into shapes so the monks could freeze the plainchant out of time, store it, and sing it back to life. ... chironomically.

Do keep up. Chironomy is the art of gesticulation or mime.[10]

---

[10] The original meaning of cheironomy as an art of bodily gesticulation, not confined to hands and arms as suggested by the Greek name, should be considered. The latter term was itself probably coined by taking the most striking part for the whole. It is not surprising, therefore, to find that in the Jewish tradition the head and the back as well as the hands are employed in spatial writing. Their respective functions are clearly defined. Of the three, the hand is the proper didactic medium for elementary teaching in religious schools (cheder)... Here is the place of the didactic hand 'waving' and 'winking' (neuma) used by the teacher to indicate the general outlines of the melody, and – even more so – its continuous flow and its animated spirituality (pneuma)'.

from the *New Grove Dictionary of Musical Instruments*, MacMillan, 1984, quoted in Ciaran Carson, *Last Night's Fun, A Book About Irish Traditional Music*, Cape, 1996.

The monks would trace the sacred words in the air as they sang, hands wafting incense, deploying pitch and rhythm in space. Let's extend the word 'neumes' here to name those gestures.

There are few things that divide poets more than the concept of rhythm, and deaf poets are no exception. Clayton Valli even encountered a number of excessively politically correct (hearing) students in one of his workshops who objected that his lecture on rhythm was 'inappropriate'. But surely rhythm is far too complex and wide-ranging a phenomenon to limit to its auditory aspect. There's a convincing argument that poetic rhythm precedes both our visual *and* auditory fields, that it's innate, hard-wired into our brains: *The Neural Lyre*, a bizarre and wonderful collaborative study by poet Frederick Turner and scientist Ernst Poppel, claims nothing less than a vindication of regular poetic metre in terms of brain physiology. Inspired by recent discoveries in human cortical information processing that the left hemisphere of the brain maps spatial information into a temporal order while the right hemisphere maps temporal information onto a spatial order, they argue that metre is in part a way of introducing right-brain processes into the left-brain activity of understanding language. Furthermore, they say, the brain possesses an auditory information 'buffer' of three seconds' worth of information (There! Now you know how long the present is!) and that this corresponds to a culturally universal and fundamental unit of metered poetry they call a LINE. In all the world's poetry, from Japanese to Ndembu (Zambia) to English, this unit falls within a 2.20 to 3 second cognitive cycle.

Obviously, this essay appeals to me on the level of strangeness and beauty. Since antiquity, poets and critics have sought to describe verse in terms of the living body – the 'organic analogy' and its related values of coherence, integration, synthesis and closure.

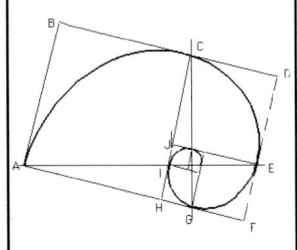

Take the celebrated number sequence discovered by Leonardo Fibonacci of Pisa in 1202 – starting at 1, each subsequent number is the sum of the two preceding numbers (1,2,3,5,8,13,21,etc...). Dividing each number in the series by the one which precedes it produces a ratio stabilising around 1.618034:, also known as the Golden Mean, the ideal proportion beloved of classical and Renaissance painters and architects, and which occurs as a logarithmic spiral in countless natural forms such as the conch shell, the arrangement of leaf stems on the stalks of plants, and the spiral distribution of seeds in the heads of sunflowers. The American poet John Frederick Nims has argued that this same ratio conforms to the original proportions of the Petrarchan sonnet. (Question: Is the sonnet built on the Renaissance sense of classical proportion or did it evolve naturally, out of the innate ordering principles of our minds?)[11] Even the most tedious and unmusical poets and critics of the 20th century have sought to justify their sense of form by organic analogy: that the line corresponds to breath, or iambic metre to the heartbeat. Paul Lake argues that conventional forms like sonnets and villanelles 'evolve, like plants, through a process of

---

[11] The trouble with this neat theory is that the sonnet would need to stop at 13 lines to fit the Golden Mean. Scottish poet Don Paterson provides an ingenious way of saving this play by moving the goalposts: 'Let me run this one by you: one and thirteen are the same number. We often use the number twelve to indicate a cycle, so that the 13th instance of something brings us back to the positiion of the first, one cycle further on; think, for example, of the hours on the clock, the months in the year, the notes in the scale. The thirteen-line sonnet is symbolic of both transformation and unity – we've returned to precisely the same point as we started but have ascended in pitch or moved forward in time: so in the song's singing, in the idea's thinking, it's transformed, but stays the same'. (Don Paterson, *101 Sonnets: From Shakespeare to Heaney*, Faber, 1999).

iteration and feedback. The regular meter of formal poems is not a dull mechanical ticking, like a clock's; it coalesces out of the rhythms of randomly jotted phrases through a process of 'phase-locking' – a natural process that occurs ...when many individual oscillators shift from a state of collective chaos to beating together or resonating in harmony... the way the randomly flickering lights of fireflies become synchronous throughout a whole tree, and the way the menstrual cycles of women living in close proximity often phase-lock into a single, collective rhythm'. [From Paul Lake's 'The Shape of Poetry' on Arthur Mortenson's website *Expansive Poetry and Music Online*.]

Cough. Let us draw a curtain across this line of inquiry and move on.

3 In and out of the frame

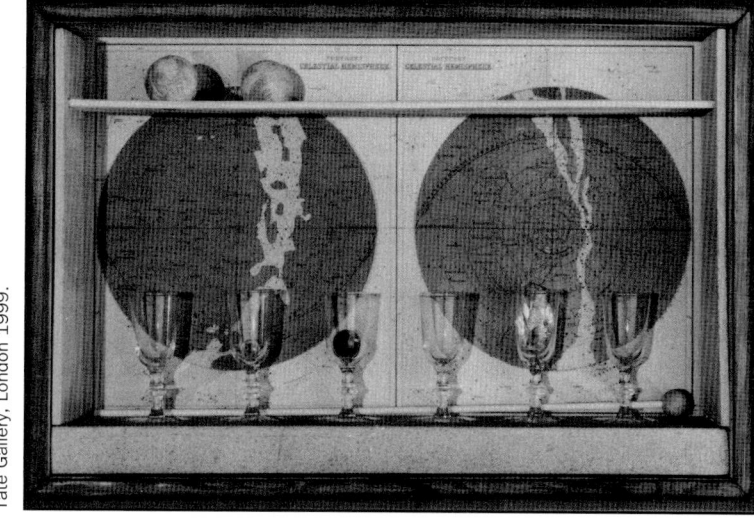

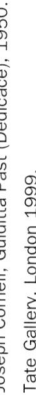
Joseph Cornell, Guiditta Past (Dedicace), 1950. Tate Gallery, London 1999.

CONSIDER NOW THE work of the American artist Joseph Cornell: a self-taught slightly mad introvert from New York, he worked in surreal miniature dioramas, arranging his materials – trinkets from Woolworths, children's handbooks of Astronomy and Birds, thimbles and seashells and broken crystals – into intimate, mysterious shadow boxes. Perhaps because of the way he synthesised his materials within the enclosure of the box so that it became a little theatre or *stanza*, critics have often called his work 'poetic'.

Academics use the word 'closure' to mean the strategies poets use to give their poems a sense of conclusion – the big build-up at the end, the clinching rhyme. I use the term '*en*closure' to describe the way in which a poem is established as All-One-Thing. In Joyce's *A Portrait of the Artist As A Young Man*, Stephen Dedalus, out for a walk with his friend Lynch points to a basket a butcher's boy is carrying and uses it to propound a theory of art based on a phrase from Aquinas: *Ad pulcritudinem tria requiruntur integritas, consonantia, claritas* ('Three things are necessary for beauty, wholeness, harmony, and radiance').

> – In order to see that basket, said Stephen, your mind first of all separates the basket from the rest of the visible universe which is not the basket. The first phase of apprehension is a bounding line drawn about the object to be apprehended. An esthetic image is presented to us either in space or in time. What is audible is presented in time, what is visible is presented in space. But, temporal or spatial, the esthetic image is first luminously apprehended as selfbounded and selfcontained upon the immeasurable background of space or time which is not it. You apprehend it as *one* thing. You see it as one whole. You apprehend its wholeness. That is *integritas*....

Enclosure in poetry is that 'bounding line drawn about the object to be apprehended' and the first step to what Joyce calls 'radiance'. Poets often play with the boundaries of the poem, exploiting an irresistible human instinct: just as we stare ink blots in a Rorschach test into the shapes of clouds or people or animals, we long to wrest coherence and integration from the structure of a poem. And as readers we're willing to go more than halfway to accommodate the poet.

A further word on frames: by an accident of typography the printed poem is traditionally laid out as a block of text in the centre of the page. This frame reinforces the impression that every poem aspires to a rectilinear condition, the shape of a mirror or a window. Windows show us the world outside our rooms, but when night falls and we switch on the lights we see only ourselves reflected in the dark glass, and sometimes, briefly, we mistake our own image for a presence outside. Mirrors, on the other hand, show us ourselves, but years on when the silver backing wears away we see past ourselves to whatever lies beyond.

So it is with poems: in our unconscious desire to locate the presence of the poet behind the frame of the words, we try to animate the poem itself (the organic analogy, see section II, above) and the poem itself seems to be *returning* our attention, or we attempt to breathe life into the inanimate.

Borges shows us a knife:

> A dagger rests in a drawer.
> It was forged in Toledo at the end of the last century. Luis Melián
>   Lafinur gave it to my father, who brought it from
>   Uruguay. Evaristo Carriego once held it in his hand.
> Whoever lays eyes on it has to pick up the dagger and toy with it,
>   as if he had always been on the lookout for it. The
>   hand is quick to grip the waiting hilt, and the
>   powerful obeying blade slides in and out of the sheath
>   with a click.
> This is not what the dagger wants.
> It is more than a structure of metal; men conceived it and shaped

> it with a single end in mind. It is, in some eternal way,
> the dagger that last night knifed a man in Tacuarembó
> and the daggers that rained on Caesar. It wants to kill,
> it wants to shed sudden blood.
> In a drawer of my writing table, among draft pages and old letters,
> the dagger dreams over and over its simple tiger's
> dream. On wielding it the hand comes alive because
> the metal comes alive, sensing itself, each time
> handled, in touch with the killer for whom it was
> forged.
> At times I am sorry for it. Such power and single-mindedness, so
> impassive or innocent its pride, and the years slip by,
> unheeding.
>
> ('The Dagger', trans. Norman Thomas Di Giovanni)

And here's another knife, wielded this time by Elizabeth Bishop (speaking in the guise of Robinson Crusoe in her dramatic monologue 'Crusoe in England'. This is an excerpt from the end of the poem)

> Now I live here, another island,
> that doesn't seem like one, but who decides?
> My blood was full of them; my brain
> bred islands. But that archipelago
> has petered out. I'm old.
> I'm bored too, drinking my real tea,
> surrounded by uninteresting lumber.

> The knife there on the shelf –
> it reeked of meaning, like a crucifix.
> It lived. How many years did I
> beg it implore it, not to break?
> I knew each nick and scratch by heart,
> the bluish blade, the broken tip,
> the lines of wood grain on the handle...
> Now it won't look at me at all.
> The living soul has dribbled away.
> My eyes rest on it and pass on.

'It reeked of meaning like a crucifix', 'It lived', but now 'it won't look at me at all'. Consider those two notes: the numinous and the animate (it looks or does not look at you). One can't help but remember here the closing lines of Rilke's great poem The Archaic Torso of Apollo: 'For here there is no place that doesn't see you. / You must change your life'.

Now there's a common species of lyric poem which takes as it's organizing principle a single dominant object called, depending on which corridor of literary history you're exploring, an image, emblem, or conceit. With the reader's permission, I'd like to introduce the term *talisman* to describe the objects we've been discussing, because it carries a suggestion of that original, pre-literate animist mentality where poetry, mnemonics and magic are mixed together.

I haven't yet forgiven you for 'neumes'.

Exactly. The *neume* is the gesture or flourish with which the poet produces the *talisman*. There's a species of modern poem that can trace its ancestry to the still life in painting – W.C. Williams'

So much depends...

Just trying to help.

so much depends

upon

a red wheel

barrow

glazed with rain

water

beside the white

chickens

famous red wheelbarrow of 1923, for example.

Look, do you mind? I know it's your brief, but these interruptions are playing havoc with the flawless architecture of my argument.

This species of poem arose, I think, in reaction to the romantic lyric in which the poet's emotions were the subject of the poem. Of course, in Williams' poem, they still are. 'So much depends' upon this ordinary object but for whom does it depend? The emotionally charged inanimate object is a commonplace of 20th century verse in English, indicative, perhaps, of a retreat from abstract nouns like *honour* and *valour* in the wake of the Great War. As Williams himself cautioned, 'No ideas but in things'.

Modern poets often build their poems about a single point of emotional focus analogous to a point of optical focus in photographs – often represented by a single object held, like Yorick's skull, in the poet's hand, a magician's prop toward which we direct our attention so that the magic can proceed by sleight of hand.[12]

---

[12] In psychoanalytic terms this object has an infantile precedent in what D. W. Winnicott calls the 'transitional object'. Most infants have a bit of old rag, blanket, particular doll or teddy bear which they cherish for months or years. Winnicott argues that these objects help us mediate, in developmental terms, between the experience of self and non-self. It's our first metaphor, invested with the power of the breast. Furthermore, says Winnicott, the mental space it occupies for us is neither subjective nor objective but 'there is the third part of the life of a human being, a part that we cannot ignore, an intermediate *area* [my italics] of experiencing, to which inner reality and external life both contribute. It is an area which is not challenged, because no claim is made on its behalf except that it shall exist as a resting place for the individual engaged in the perpetual human task of keeping inner and outer reality separate yet inter-related' (1950, p230). For Winnicott, all art begins in the transitional phenomena of infancy, the zone between subjectivity and objectivity (see D. W. Winnicott, *Playing and Reality*, and my second digression, below).

4 When I snap my fingers you will open your eyes

IT IS AN ANCIENT MARINER… The illusion of the physical presence of the poet depends on the illusion of the present moment of the poem, a moment in which the poet can assert his or her presence. Look at this watch. If I press this, a spring mechanism flicks open its heavily tarnished gold plated lid.

Chironomy again. With such modest gestures the poet opens up a little world for the poem.

It's precisely here that the poet creates the illusion of the poem's moment. On a particular day, in a particular room, a poet holds on his palm a particular object:

We find ourselves beside a fire in the lobby of a hotel in Eastbourne. Mr Donaghy has shown us this watch before.

Timer

Gold survives the fire that's hot enough
to make you ashes in a standard urn.
An envelope of coarse official buff
contains your wedding ring which wouldn't burn..

Dad told me I'd to tell them at St James's
that the ring should go in the incinerator.
That 'eternity' inscribed with both their names is
his surety that they'd be together 'later'.

I signed for the parcelled clothing as the son,

33

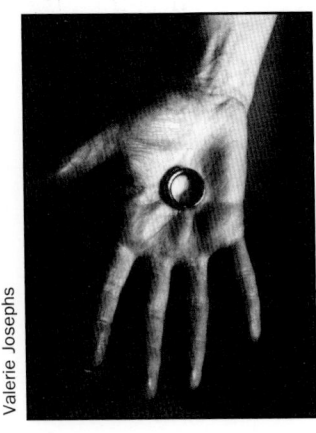

Valerie Josephs

| present |
| past |
| past |
| present |

the cardy, apron, pants, bra, dress

the clerk phoned down: 6-8-8-3-1 ?
Has she still her ring on? (Slight pause) Yes!

It's on my warm palm now, your burnished ring.

I feel your ashes, head, arms, breasts, womb, legs
sift through its circle slowly, like that thing
you used to let me watch to time the eggs.

    Here Tony Harrison performs a kind of magic trick, transforming, by sleight of hand, his mother's wedding ring into the narrow 'waist' of an egg timer (the tiny domestic descendant of that venerable symbol of mortality, the hourglass) See what he's done? Watch again.

    The poem begins in the present tense and the second person, addressed to 'you'. For a split second we may believe he's addressing his reader, or employing a universal 'you' – 'to make one ashes…'. But when he shifts back to the immediate past in the second stanza it's clear he's invoking a common convention of the elegiac lyric, permitting us to eavesdrop as he talks to his dead mother. In the third quatrain (for this is a symmetrical poem of four four line stanzas with two purely visual breaks for dramatic emphasis) he describes how her mortal form was degraded by death, reduced to a parcel of garments and a number. When he asks the clerk if '6-8-8-3-1', formerly Mrs. Harrison, is still wearing the ring, he gives us a dramatic stage direction '(Slight Pause)' in which we're invited to imagine, as the grieving son must, the faceless stranger on the end of the phone line inspecting his mother's naked corpse. And now the sleight of hand: Harrison switches back to the present tense and establishes the imaginary moment of the poem by showing us the object of the poem, the talisman, the ring. But we arrive back at the title by way of a heartbreaking simile, an intimate childhood memory, for the 'timer', not the ring, is the true focus of the son's grief. The ring is inscribed with 'eternity', together with 'surety' the only abstract nouns in the poem, but the timer evokes impermanence. Analysed in this way, Harrison's poem is just so much sideshow trickery, but while we watch his hands he works something akin to true magic. He moves us.

Harrison establishes his poem's enclosure with traditional techniques of rhyme and metre and chiastic structure. Now let's watch another magician, one who uses an altogether different principle of enclosure. Keep your eye on the cup:

The Story of The White Cup
for Helen

I am not sure why I want to tell it
since the cup was not mine and I was not there,
and it may not have been white after all.
When I tell it, though, it is white, and the girl
to whom it has just been given, by her mother,
is eight. She is holding a white cup against her breast,
and her mother has just said goodbye, though those
could not have been, exactly, the words. No one knows

what her father has said, but when I tell it,
he is either helping someone very old with a bag,
a worn valise held in place with a rope,
or asking a guard for a cigarette. There is, of course,
no cigarette. The cattle cars stand with their doors
slid back. They are black inside, and the girl
who has just been given a cup and told to walk
in a straight line and told to look like she wants
a drink of water, who screamed in the truck
all the way to the station, who knew, at eight,
where she was going, is holding a cup to her breast
and walking away, going nowhere, for water.
She does not turn, but when she has found water,
which she does, in all versions of the story, everywhere,
she takes a small sip of it, and swallows.

voice

story

cup

Here the American poet Roger Mitchell blocks our habituated emotional responses, our escapes into historical abstraction, sentimentality, or that media-generated phenomenon, 'compassion fatigue', by a formal subterfuge. We can't possibly know where and when the 'story of the white cup' takes place until we encounter the words 'cattle cars' – halfway through the poem, when we're in too deep to back out. Even the title is strategically misleading, for this is the story *of the story* of the white cup. Like Coleridge, Mitchell has interposed a voice compelled to bear witness, 'I am not sure why I want to tell it', a formula that might as easily imply indolence as urgency. The style is studied artlessness – no similes, no metaphors, no discernible poetic diction – but the storyteller must offer us specificity, *focus*, or the story evaporates, so he fills in the gaps 'When I tell it, though, it is white' informing us at every stage of his decisions: 'but when I tell it, / he is either helping someone very old with a bag, / a worn valise held in place with a rope, / or asking a guard for a cigarette'. 'Bag', of course, is blurry, so he slowly twists his lens to a sharper image, to more information, to the desperation and fear implied by the incongruous 'valise' (US, overnight bag) overpacked and held shut by a rope. But whatever its colour, the one object beyond fabrication is the cup, the talisman at the centre of the story, a story framed by voice, a voice framed by the poem. And it's the cup that locates us in the present of a German or Polish railway station in, say, 1942, in the *presence* of the poem. Because in Mitchell's 'telling' the past tense is transmuted at every point into the present – *I am telling it....it is white*.

I defer here to the magus of unsupported assertion, Ezra Pound, who famously defined his version of the image as 'that which presents an intellectual and emotional complex in an instant of time'. That 'instant' reminds me of 'instamatic', and of the documentary truth of the snapshot (and George Eastman had sold his first Brownie only a decade before). A Grecian urn may well represent an 'intellectual and emotional complex', but an 'instant' can focus an allegorical vessel floating in eternity into a teacup in Bloomsbury in 1913. But half a century earlier we can watch another magician use a similar strategy to describe time in spatial terms whilst casually obliterating an oaf with an eagle feather.[13]

Memorabilia

Ah, did you once see Shelley plain,
And did he stop and speak to you?
And did you speak to him again?
How strange it seems, and new!

But you were living before that,
And you are living after,
And the memory I started at –
My starting moves your laughter!

I crossed a moor, with a name of its own
And a certain use in the world no doubt,
Yet a hand's-breadth of it shines alone
'Mid the blank miles round about:

For there I picked up on the heather
And there I put inside my breast
A moulted feather, an eagle-feather –
Well, I forget the rest.

---

[13] 'The left hemisphere of the brain maps spatial information into a temporal order while the right hemispere maps temporal information onto a spatial order'. Jerre Levy, quoted by Turner and Pöppel, quoted in *Wallflowers, a lecture on poetry, with misplaced notes and additional heckling*, Michael Donaghy, London 1999. They continue: 'The fact that experienced musicians use their left brain just as much as their right in listening to music shows that their higher understanding of music is the result of the collaboration of both "brains", the music having been translated first from temporal sequence to spatial pattern, and then "read back into a temporal movement"'.

I'm just as struck by the sheer venom of this little poem as I am by its modernity. Browning is reported to have related 'with characteristic vehemence "I was one day in the shop of Hodgson, the well known London bookseller, when a stranger...spoke of something that Shelley had once said to him. Suddenly the stranger paused, and burst into laughter as he observed me staring at him with blanched face... I still vividly remember how strangely the presence of a man who had seen and spoken with Shelley affected me"'. The present moment of the poem is represented here by that dash after 'at' in line seven when he interrupts himself – as though he were being interrupted again by the stranger's laughter – and again in line fifteen, before delivering his withering *coup de grace*. At which point, I think, we're supposed to imagine Browning, or Browning's stunt man, turning on his heels leaving the speechless recipient contemplating his kinship to a stretch of unremarkable moorland. For that's the principal metaphor of this poem; *time* – an incident in a stranger's life, a few words with the author of 'The Triumph of Life' – equated with *space* – a hand's-breadth of moor occupied by a feather. But we only arrive at this conclusion by way of a secondary equation, when we return to a gesture performed in time, a neume and talisman (forgive me) when Browning slips the feather in his pocket. Pardon me. An *eagle* feather in his *breast*. For these are venerable emblems: the eagle, of power and isolate majesty, the feather, or quill, of the scribe or poet, the breast, of the house of the soul. He has taken this second-hand glimpse of Shelley to his heart. And then?

Nothing. Browning 'forgets the rest' he tells us in the last line of the poem, which, as all good poets know, is the line designed to send the reader's eye back to the title. 'Memorabilia' retains both the mnemonic meaning of rhetorical points or images to be remembered as well as the ordinary sense of the bric a brac and relics of fame, and Browning marries both meanings here. The apparent modernity of the poem, Browning's abrupt excursion into the countryside, owes nothing to any theory, programme or manifesto. It's simply a matter of wit, timing and performance. 'Sir', he might have said, 'you may have a name, and a use in the world, *no doubt*, but you are clearly not the *subject* of this poem'.

Second digression

Before we go any further it may very well have occurred to you that I've been throwing the words 'subject' and 'object' about with abandon. To clear things up let's check the etymology of these abstract terms. Not surprisingly, they started life as physical actions. 'Object' comes from *objectus*, past participle of of *obicere* 'to throw in the way, prevent, hinder', from *ob-* in the way + *jacere* to throw. 'Subject' derives from *subjectus*, pp. of *subicere*, 'to throw under'. No ideas but in neumes, and as the above examples show, all abstraction in language and thought is a system of concrete metaphors unanchored from their roots in the physical world. Even as basic an abstraction as the verb 'to be' is rooted in the Sanskrit *bhu*, 'to grow' whereas 'am' and 'is' share a root with the Sanskrit *asmi*, 'to breathe'.

As a noun, my dictionary defines 'object' as 1) something material that may be perceived by the senses: 'I see an object in the distance'; 2) something mental or physical toward which thought, feeling, or action is directed 'an object for study' or a 'meticulously carved art object' and 3) the goal or end of an effort or activity, a purpose, objective.

For 'subject' we have, first, the mind, ego, or agent that sustains thought or consciousness; 2) one that is acted upon; 3) an individual whose reactions or responses are studied; 4) something concerning which something is said or done 'the subject of the study' 5) something represented or indicated in a work of art.[14]

Clearly, there's a grey area where the word subject will do as well as object. In becoming art, all objects become subjects, that is, they are mediated – whether represented or merely presented by the consciousness of the poet. The neumes and talismans I see in so many lyric poems, the imaginary moment outside time in which the audience focuses on the poet's hand, and, in that hand, the ring, cup, feather, knife, ' bracelet of bright hair about the bone' the moment in which that talisman becomes a living presence... all these have as their precedent the central ritual gesture of European

---

[14] I'd prepared much of the present lecture when I received this e-mail from a friend at the Arts Council whose judgement I respect above my own. [1a]

MD –

Re your essay Wallflowers on poetry and the poetry reader: For my part I find the argument, insofar as it can be classed an argument at all, reasonably accessible. But the style – especially for an oral presentation, is entirely too cluttered. At times I felt I was navigating through some dark dance club packed with gyrating ravers and my friends had gone missing and the strobe lights were hammering away on my retinas. In short, what I had supposed substances were thinned away into shadows, while everywhere shadows were deepened into substances.

Rest assured, though, that I look forward to your book on Bruno, Coleridge, Yeats and Joyce which you've been threatening to write since 1977. Save the metaphysics for that future project,. If you take this direction in the present lecture, the event will extend for several days. And as far as publishing a lecture of such a length... well, funds are limited.

Best of luck anyway,

– RJL

I couldn't argue with this, so I'll content myself for the present with sketching the conclusions of a carefully constructed argument which I have reserved for that future publication.

[1a] Well I would.

civilization these past two millenia – the elevation of the host in the sacrifice of the Mass.

End of digression

5 In Lieu of a Conclusion

Readers, I appeal to you! 'Mr Donaghy', as the words on the right insist on calling themselves, is a mirage. These words, however, are entirely your own. Pay no attention to that man behind the curtain!

TIME'S UP. LET me finish, if not conclude, with a few quotable memorabilia. First, twentieth century literary poetry has been at war with itself and its readers. Secondly, this has not been an unalloyed boon. By attacking traditional terms of engagement with the audience, modernist poets and critics at once cut poetry's lifeline to the oral tradition and developed immeasurably our capacity to think speculatively and innovatively about the genre. But now that the century's up, how do we re-engage with poems?

Memorise. When we learn a dance step, a part in a play, a song, or a poem by heart, we give it a body to live in. We own a poem, or at least our expression of it, in a profoundly deeper way than is possible if it's stored away on a page. But why is this desirable? If poetry is merely a sophisticated cultural toy, or a commodified entertainment, it's a pointless exercise. But if you're reading this essay, chances are you already believe that a great poem is in some sense a repository of wisdom, or wonder, or presence, if only by virtue of its own excellence. If its words are ingrained in our memories they're constantly available to our unconscious, like a computer program running in the background. If its words are inscribed on our hearts, they can guide us out of our emptiness. Time's up.

6 Concluding Neume

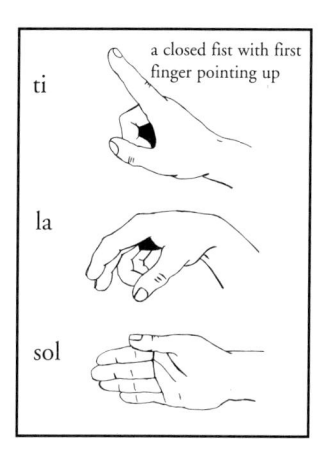

ti	a closed fist with first finger pointing up
la	
sol	

JOHN KEATS HOLDS out his hand:

This living hand, now warm and capable
Of earnest grasping, would, if it were cold
And in the icy silence of the tomb,
So haunt thy days and chill thy dreaming nights
That thou wouldst wish thine own heart dry of blood
So in my veins red life might stream again,
And thou be conscience-calmed – see here it is –
I hold it towards you.

In his loneliness and fixedness he yearneth towards the journeying Moon, and the stars that still sojourn, yet still move onward; and every where the blue sky belongs to them, and is their appointed rest, and their native country and their own natural homes, which they enter unannounced, as lords that are certainly expected and yet there is a silent joy at their arrival.

Acknowledgements

IMAGINE GROWING UP in a society where one's first and only experience of music occurred in a schoolroom, where the beauty of music was meticulously analysed and explained to you and where you were judged by your ability to explain it in turn. In one sense your appreciation of music would be exquisitely sophisticated because tunes wouldn't be tinkling persistently out of lift speakers or commuters' headphones. Music wouldn't be an 'on' switch away, so you'd be more alert to its nuances when you did hear it. But let's face it, you wouldn't be queuing round the corner for the experience. It would always be more 'improving' than pleasurable. Well that's more or less our (urban, educated, Anglophone) experience of poetry. Perhaps its low profile has to do with the way it's taught. On the graduate level, modern pedagogues have long felt disinclined to lead tour groups around the gallery waving their pointing sticks at the sheer genius of the Old Masters. They want to be the main event. Literacy corrupts, they seem to be saying, and Literature, the common ground of writing agreed to be worthy of survival, is the tool of the oppressor. If poetry depended on intellectuals for its survival it would about as current as hieroglyphics.

They exhibit common scholarly errors of reading from the outside, of treating the 'canon' as as a corpse to be wheeled out for dissection practice by generations of medical students. Literary taste was effectively banished from the curriculum when I was a student. I remember complaining that a particular contemporary poet we were studying wasn't to my taste. The professor looked baffled. 'Taste?' he laughed and pointed to his tongue, 'Taste is here.' I was

47

pleasantly surprised when another professor – James K. Chandler – read Coleridge's 'Frost at Midnight' aloud, all 567 words of it, paused, and asked us if we thought it was beautiful. Thanks, Jim. That's the only time in my experience of academe I got any indication that it might be relevant to find pleasure in a poem.

For the past year I've been 'reader-in-residence' for the Poetry Society. I tried the opposite approach, running discussions and 'close-readings' of poems, mostly with groups of librarians, in which we tried to understand the poem from a maker's point of view. In other words, I followed the example set by schools of music and painting, where criticism and theory are taught in conjunction with practice. If your only experience of motoring lay in deconstructing the Highway Code you could hardly be expected to understand the allure of the automobile, so I took my readers for a spin round the block.

My principal accomplishment in this post, however, lay in organising my ideas about poetry into this disgracefully disorganised 'lecture', I'm grateful to the Poetry Society and the Arts Council for giving me the opportunity to do this. Some of the ideas came out of conversations with Chris Meade, Don Paterson, Sean O'Brien, Colin Falck, and – especially – Jo Shapcott. Special thanks to Stephen Troussé for his patience with my eleventh hour changes and his flair for design, to Christina Patterson for her record-breaking final lap dash to obtain rights and permissions, to Maddy Paxman for her speedy proof-reading, and to Eammon Shanahan for his help in obtaining elusive material.

MICHAEL DONAGHY